A VISION OF AEROPLANES

A Motet for Mixed Choir (SATB) and Organ

words from Ezekiel, Chapter I
music by R. Vaughan Williams

OXFORD

UNIVERSITY PRESS

A Vision of Aeroplanes

I looked, and, behold, a whirlwind came out of the north, a great cloud, and a fire infolding itself, and a brightness was about it, and out of the midst thereof as the colour of amber, out of the midst of the fire. Also out of the midst thereof came the likeness of four living creatures. And this was their appearance; they had the likeness of a man. And every one had four faces, and every one had four wings . . . . . . their wings were joined one to another; they turned not when they went; they went everyone straight forward; . . . . they went every one straight forward; whither the spirit was to go, they went; and they turned not when they went . . . . . Their appearance was like burning coals of fire and like the appearance of lamps; it went up and down among the living creatures; and the fire was bright, and out of the fire went forth lightning. And the living creatures ran and returned as the appearance of a flash of lightning.

Now as I beheld the living creatures, behold one wheel upon the earth by the living creatures with his four faces . . . . . Their appearance and their work was, as it were, a wheel in the middle of a wheel. When they went, they went upon their four sides: and they turned not when they went. As for their rings, they were so high they were dreadful: and their rings were full of eyes round about them four. And when the living creatures went, the wheels went by them: and when the living creatures were lifted up from the earth, the wheels were lifted up, ... when those went, these went; and when those stood, these stood; and when those were lifted up from the earth, the wheels were lifted up over against them: for the spirit of the living creature was in the wheels . . . . . .

And when they went, I heard the noise of their wings, like the noise of great waters, as the voice of the Almighty . . . . . . when they stood, they let down their wings and there was a voice from the firmament that was over their heads, when they stood, and had let down their wings.

And above the firmament that was over their heads was the likeness of a throne, as the appearance of a sapphire stone; and upon the likeness of the throne was the likeness as the appearance of a man . . . . . . This was the appearance of the likeness of the glory of the Lord. And when I saw it I fell upon my face.

Ezekiel, Chapter I

A Vision of Aeroplanes

From Ezekiel, Chapter I

R. VAUGHAN WILLIAMS

Duration: about 15 minutes

Printed in Great Britain

4

*The Tenor line should include a few high Baritones. When the Tenor parts rise above F an alternative note is added for use by the Baritones.

A Vision of Aeroplanes

bright - ness was a-bout it, ___ and out ___ of the midst there -

bright - ness was a-bout it, ___ and out ___ of the midst there -

bright - ness was a-bout it, ___ and out ___ of the midst there -

bright - ness was a-bout it, ___ and out ___ of the midst there -

-of as the col - our of am - - - ber,

-of as the col - our of am - - - ber,

- of as the col - our of am - - - ber,

-of as the col - our of am - - - ber,

A Vision of Aeroplanes

A Vision of Aeroplanes

wings were joined one ___ to an-oth-er; they turned not when they went; they went

wings were joined one ___ to an-oth-er; they turned not when they went; they went

wings were joined one ___ to an-oth-er; they turned not when they went; they went

wings were joined one ___ to an-oth-er; they turned not when they went; they went

ev - e-ry one straight for - ward; they

ev - - e-ry one straight for-ward;

ev - - - e-ry one straight for - ward;

ev - - - - - - e-ry one straight

A Vision of Aeroplanes

A Vision of Aeroplanes

16

A Vision of Aeroplanes

A Vision of Aeroplanes

And when the liv-ing crea - tures went,____ the wheels went

And when the liv-ing crea - tures went,____ the wheels went

by them: and when the liv-ing crea -

by them: and when the liv-ing crea -

- tures were lift-ed up from the earth, the wheels____ were____

- tures were lift-ed up from the earth, the wheels____ were____

A Vision of Aeroplanes

A Vision of Aeroplanes

22

A Vision of Aeroplanes

A Vision of Aeroplanes

A Vision of Aeroplanes

26

A Vision of Aeroplanes

OXFORD
UNIVERSITY PRESS

www.oup.com

ISBN 978-0-19-385678-3

9 780193 856783